How We Got Here

I prayed to God, asking Him how I could honor my wife (1 Peter 3:7) for all that she does. This is what He gave me. Welcome to the past 5 years of our life…

Today she stood up for me and had my back. she said that my advice was biblical, and that really meant a lot to me knowing she is there to support me.

Who can find a virtuous and capable wife? She is more precious than rubies.

On Sunday, she woke up early and made me breakfast, and at the same time watched Eli so that I could sleep in before church.

Her husband can trust her, and she will greatly enrich his life.

today I had to work 9 hours and drive 4 hours after work. I got home and was not the happiest person. She was pretty understanding about me being grumpy. She's awesome.

She brings him good, not harm, all the days of her life.

My wife is the best because my mom was sick and my wife went to the store, went over to my mom's house, and then made her chicken noodle soup.

She finds wool and flax and busily spins it.

Story

Tonight, my wife warmed up leftovers for dinner and it was spoiled. She immediately made breakfast burritos for the both of us. She's pretty great.

Proverbs 31:14

She is like a merchant's ship, bringing her food from afar.

My wife is so great because even when she hates making my lunches, she still does it for me every day. Love is a choice and many times, she chooses to love me regardless of how she feels. I pray God blesses her for that.

She gets up before dawn to prepare breakfast for her household and plan the day's work for her servant girls.

My wife was so kind today. Her self-control and respect really blessed my day in a way that made me so thankful for her. I know it's not easy having me as her other half but God has given my wife understanding and I love my life.

She goes to inspect a field and buys it; with her earnings she plants a vineyard.

Baby boy was not having a good day. Probably was his teeth. Mom was brilliant. She knew time after time just what to do to help him make it through the day. My wife is such a blessing to both me and my son.

She is energetic and strong, a hard worker.

Almost every day when I get home, my wife has food hot and ready for me. I pray God blesses her for taking care of this family.

She makes sure her dealings are profitable; her lamp burns late into the night.

I worked Monday - Friday and throughout the entire holiday weekend, I was hunting and scouting. My wife watched my son for a week straight and didn't complain really once. I know it's tough on her with Eli being so needy at this age. My wife is the best.

Her hands are
busy spinning
thread,
her fingers twisting
fiber.

I kind of have been bugging my wife lately and I know it's been tough on her, dealing with all of my nonsense, but she continues to put herself aside and help me out as much as she can. I know that God is in her heart because if He wasn't, then she couldn't love me as much as she does. I am more than blessed to have such a wife.

She extends a helping hand to the poor and opens her arms to the needy.

My wife was kind of irritated after church on Sunday. I mentioned that she should change her attitude. SHE DID! It doesn't work like that all the time, but I was so thankful today that she did. Praise God that I have a wife who tries her best (with the help of God) to be an amazing wife.

She has no fear of winter for her household, for everyone has warm clothes.

My son's first birthday. I over ate the day before, was pooping and throwing up; not sleeping. While I watched Eli, she took care of everything and it was a really great birthday for him. She is great. She also yelled at me lol.

She makes her own bedspreads. She dresses in fine linen and purple gowns.

I can't explain this feeling but I'll explain the situation. My sister-in-law is throwing a birthday party for my nephew. My brother said I am not welcomed at his house. My wife chose not to attend because I'm not welcome. Furthermore, she still told my sister-in-law that she would make the cakes and cupcakes for the party. To do something kind even when being insulted or offended...only by the hand of God. I am so blessed to have such a forgiving, kind wife that stands by my side

I don't even know what to say. I felt like I wanted to say something amazing that my wife is doing but I can't speak to just one single thing because she is and has been in every aspect of my life, consistently doing and saying things to strengthen my relationship with God, our marriage, and as a family. She is so great and I am so blessed.

Her husband is well known at the city gates, where he sits with the other civic leaders.

I got home yesterday, my wife had dinner ready, and even prepared my food for the next day. she gave baby a bath, tried her best to listen as we read the Bible with baby trying not to explode with energy, and then she put baby to sleep. She blesses my life and takes care of this household.

Proverbs 31:24

She makes belted linen garments and sashes to sell to the merchants.

I get wrapped up in materialistic things and want to buy expensive toys. glad God gave me a helper to keep me from buying everything I want to. The flesh is never satisfied. Thankful for my wife to help keep me on track.

She is clothed with strength and dignity,
and she laughs without fear of the future.

Out of the kindness of her heart, my wife gives food to Emo. He never says thanks or even asks and my wife continues to generously give him food. I pray God blesses her for it and that she continues to show/ help me become better. God sure did give me a good one.

When she speaks, her words are wise, and she gives instructions with kindness.

I am so blessed that God gave me a wife that prays for me. She prayed that God would keep my mouth closed at work. Praise God that he answered her and my prayer.

Proverbs 31:27

She carefully watches everything in her household and suffers nothing from laziness.

We found out that my pregnant wife has Placentia Previa and with everything else going on, ear pulsing and being pregnant, living in the travel trailer, with my 2-year-old, now the stress of this. My wife has a lot on her plate and yet she is still by my side, enduring. I am blessed to have such an amazing woman who has given her life to God.

Her children stand and bless her.
Her husband praises her.

My wife told me she's been witnessing to her cousin. and her cousin's husband. Seeing that is such a blessing. God's doing a great work through my wife because she's willing to allow Him to do so. I am very blessed to have such a wife.

There are many virtuous and capable women in the world, but you surpass them all!

Being 7.5 months pregnant, finding out she has Gestational Diabetes with the pregnancy, just getting over the complete placenta previa, and having to deal with a mischief 2-year-old and me, I asked her to try to have self-control with him and me and to build up her home instead of tear it down. It's noticeable that she's trying and I praise God for giving my wife understanding and for giving me a wife that will try to do what is right, even when it's really hard.

Dealing with the news that our daughter may be born very much underweight and retarded, dealing with the stress of being in a travel trailer and having an over active 2-year-old, and that some of her Graves Disease issues have come back, I can see her battling the mix of emotions. Although it's been really tough, she hasn't given up on all 3 of us (baby in belly), and she's working hard to eat to give baby the best chance at starting this life. I pray God blesses my wife for all that she does for this family.

New Years in the trailer with 2 sick children and 1 sick wife with it being cold outside. My wife continues to push through and take care of this family and home. things are difficult right now, but I pray God blesses my wife for all that she does.

Charm is deceptive, and beauty does not last; but a woman who fears the Lord will be greatly praised.

My wife is now watching Levi, my nephew, taking care of both our kids, and our household. She is fair and she is giving. She does a lot and does not get much in return. She has not had fun money in who knows how long and yet she still works hard and puts up with me and Eli. God really blessed me with an amazing wife.

Proverbs 31:31

Reward her for all she has done. Let her deeds publicly declare her praise.

With the house builder running off with thousands of dollars, leaving us with an unfinished home and very little money, my wife, while she was breastfeeding, laid the flooring to the entire house by herself and it looks amazing. She saved us $4,000 and kept our house project going. She said to pay her for labor costs lol. She hasn't really had spending money for herself in years. With our tax return, I was able to reward her for what she has done (Proverbs 31) with nowhere near $4,000.

Now that God alone has finished the home enough for us to live in it, we have accepted the reality that if God gave us a home, then it's because He wants us to use it to be a blessing to others. God has blessed us with the desire to show godly hospitality (which is different than entertaining) to all who come into this home and my wife has been the one to carry much, if not most, of that load. She cooks food for everyone, she cleans and makes sure it's ready for people to come over. Then, she cleans up after everyone leaves. She does so much and doesn't ask for anything in return. After, she feels so blessed to have the ability to do all of this for everyone. How is it possible that I am as blessed as I am? Only by the hand of God.

My wife has such a unique ministry. God has blessed her with such an amazing artistic talent in so many different areas and she is using those talents for the glory of God. She likes baking, so she and a few other women from church, made cupcakes for all of the single women in our church for Valentine's day. Then, on a very cold windy day, she and another lady delivered every single one of them personally to each lady at their home. She told me there were many tears between her and the other women. God is doing mighty works through my wife. I am truly blessed.

My dad had covid19, pneumonia, and a heart attack. My mom was sick. My wife took care not only of our household, but also my parents as well. Picking up prescriptions or food for my parents daily, still taking care of my children and I, and not complaining about it. My wife is such a blessing to all of those around her.

I can't recall what it was that my wife said, but she said something that was the right advice at the right time. It was so good, that I was even bragging to my friend about how much he needs to get married to a godly woman because having a godly wife (helper) helps us guys stay on the right track. There's nothing better in this life (aside from God), then a marriage done God's way. I am so thankful to God for my wife who helps me daily.

My wife is a woman who fears God. Being a year since I've started working from home because of Covid19, I haven't eaten lunch much. I asked my wife if she could start making lunch for me again even with me at home. She didn't want to, but she did anyway. I am a very blessed man to have the wife that I do. I know that God continues to bless my wife for her obedience to God.

My father has had very difficult times recently with his health. My mother has needed so much help, and my wife has been there for my children and me, and for my mom and dad. My wife has treated my father and mother as if they were her parents from birth. She has helped them physically and spiritually. She has cried with them, and she has laughed with them. My sisters and she have come together in the Lord helping my parents and have been strengthened as one body in Christ. God has truly blessed my life through this woman, all glory to God.

Part 1 - My wife is not very talkative, not even with me. However, there are times every so often that the kids will allow us to speak to each other and I get a little bit of insight into what my wife does when I'm not around. Last night she told me that she invited some girls that she didn't even know to church on Sunday. Again, she doesn't talk. That tells me that she is trusting and obeying Jesus Christ because she's doing things that she's not capable of doing by herself. I am so proud of the godly wife that the Lord has given me and thankful to God that He is surrounding my wife with godly women. I am so blessed.

Part 2 of the previous conversation with my wife, I found out that my wife was connecting people who do not know Jesus Christ as their Lord/ Savior with people who do know Jesus Christ as their Lord/ Savior. She has managed (all glory to God) to get a nonbeliever to follow the page of a believer and has noticed that the unbeliever has been reading and liking lots of Christian posts from the believer. My wife has shared in the ministry of the believer and so many seeds are being planted because of my wife's shrewdness. I pray God continues to use my wife to do His mighty works to further His kingdom. What a blessing it is to know that I have a wife who is storing up so many treasures for herself in paradise/ eternity. I don't deserve God's goodness, but He continues to give it to me, many of them through my wife.

With the difficulties in my father's health, my mother continues to be in great need. After hearing my wife on the phone with my mom, I asked her what they were talking about. She told me that she was telling my mom a funny story and how my mom started laughing so hard, it gave her a hot flash. My wife said that it seemed as though with everything that my mom is going through, that she really needed, or that it really helped her to be able to laugh like that. The Bible says that a joyful heart is good medicine and I have a wife that helps not only with her hands, but also with her words. I am so blessed to have a wife who gives my family medicine in times of need. Thank you God for my wife, and for the great works that you do through her.

Yesterday, when my wife got home from her Bible study, she told me how much she enjoyed last night's Bible study that she goes to up at our church. I don't know if there's really anything better that a husband could hear than how much joy his wife receives from fellowshipping with other believers and studying God's word. God really did give me an amazing woman and helper who truly blesses my life.

Speaking to my mom on the phone, and hearing my mom crying, put me in a place of not knowing how to react or respond. Dealing with the struggles of my dad's health situation, she said she can't do this anymore.
My wife immediately yelled at me in a quiet voice and said, pray with her! One of my weaknesses is not praying in moments when prayer is necessary. God gave me my wife to help me with that and I'm thankful for it.

My wife has really been helping at church a lot recently. She has become known as someone who has many talents and is very helpful with a lot of different things. A family in the church was looking for graduation pictures for their son and my wife was recommended to them. Not only did my wife take graduation pictures for their son, she also took family pictures, and tried to refuse payment when offered. She said, "I'm just going to donate it all to the church" lol, but the family was not having it, so she gave only a portion of it to the church as an offering and then put the rest in her gas tank (I think). She knows that God provides for our needs, always has and always will, if we seek Him first and live righteously (Matthew 6:33). Jesus Christ is our provider and sustainer, and my wife stands confidently with Him as her foundation, praise God!

Again, my wife is helping a lot up at the church. She has been asked by multiple women to help with the preparation and prayer duties for Vacation Bible School (VBS). If that's not awesome enough, before she left to go help with decorations, she made sure that a large, homemade, from scratch, chicken pot pie, fresh out of the oven, was sitting on the stove before she left. God has created and continues to create in my wife, a Proverbs 31 woman, a wife of noble character by the power of the Holy Spirit. How blessed am I that God has joined me with this godly woman; two united into one.

Summary

Truly, God has blessed me beyond what I deserve.

Proverbs 18:22

The man who finds a wife finds a treasure, and he receives favor from the LORD.

Reference

Life Application Study Bible (Large Print), New Living Translation. (2007). Tyndale House Publishers, Inc. (Original work published 1996)

All verses cited are in the New Living Translation